Cartooning

Deri Robins

QEB Publishing

Copyright © QEB Publishing, Inc 2004

Published in the United States by
QEB Publishing, Inc.
23062 La Cadena Drive
Laguna Hills
Irvine
CA 92653

Library of Congress Control Number:
2004101530

ISBN 1-59566-044-5

Written by Deri Robins
Designed by Wladek Szechter/Louise Morley
Edited by Sian Morgan/Matthew Harvey

Creative Director: Louise Morley
Editorial Manager: Jean Coppendale

Credits: Corbis /Douglas Kirkland 6t
Jack Keely: 8–9, 11, 14, 18–19, 20, 25;
Roger Armstrong: 8; Don Jardine: 14;
Ed Nofziger: 17
Jim Robins 17b

Printed and
bound in China

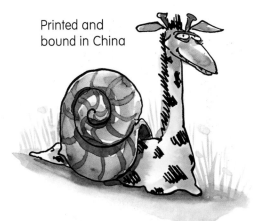

The words in **bold** are
explained in the Glossary
on page 30.

Contents

Tools and materials 4

Cartoon tips and hints 6

Cartoon figures 8

Faces and features 10

Dressing up 12

On the move 14

Cartoon creatures 16

It's alive! 18

Scary monsters 20

Set the scene 22

Comic capers 24

Make a comic 26

Making movies 28

Glossary 30

Index 31

Notes for teachers and parents 32

Tools and materials

Anyone can draw cartoons—the more you practice, the better you'll become! This book has lots of ideas to help you improve your cartooning skills, along with projects to try out at home and school.

Tools of the trade

All you really need is a pencil and plenty of paper. It's also good to experiment with as many different materials as possible. **HB** or **B** pencils are ideal for first sketches— they rub out easily. You can go over the **outlines** in pen at the end.

Cartoon experiments!

Why not try using some of the other cartooning tools? For example, markers are great for drawing big, bold cartoons. You can use felt-tips, poster paints, and inks for making bold, colorful cartoons. Colored inks and watercolors are good for soft shades. Remember, if you use paint or ink, draw your outlines in waterproof pen, or they will run when you start painting.

Paper

Use scrap paper for your rough ideas, and smooth drawing paper for your finished cartoons.

There are lots of different materials you can use to create cartoons. As you experiment with different pens, paints, and pencils, you'll see they all create different effects.

crayons

pastels

pencils

felt tips

Drawing board

You need a hard surface to support your paper when you're drawing. Use a desk or board positioned at a slight angle and keep the paper in place with masking tape or thumbtacks. You need plenty of light when you are drawing, either natural sunlight or a desk lamp.

Protect your cartoons

Artwork is easily damaged. Tape your best pictures to mount board and tape a piece of tissue paper over the top to protect it.

Keep your ideas in a notebook or sketchbook.

art paper

poster paint

colored ink

Cartoon tips

Look for cartoon inspiration at home, at school, on vacation, in the country, or at the beach. Start with a person, an animal, or an object that you know well, or use your imagination to create a fantasy character or monster.

What is a cartoon?

What makes cartoons different from other drawings? Think about your favorite cartoon character from movies, television, comic strips, or picture books.

"The Simpsons," created by Matt Groening, is known the world over.

ANIMAL MAGIC

Look carefully at different animals and make sketches of them. Real animals might not keep still for long, so look at books, magazines, or websites on the Internet. You could also watch wildlife programs on television or use a microscope to look at tiny insects.

People pictures

Look carefully at your family, friends, or favorite celebrity. Everyone has a unique **feature** that would make a great cartoon. Collect photos of people in different outfits, positions, and poses. Look at them for ideas when you draw your cartoons.

MUM

DAD

Cool cartoons

You can get different effects depending on which tools you use. Use a black pen or felt-tip to **outline** and **shade** your cartoons. Felt-tips create bold outlines and flat color. Colored inks give a softer effect. Combine a black ink outline with pencils, colored ink, or **watercolors**.

Cartoon figures

The easiest way to draw a cartoon figure is to sketch a simple **outline** first, and then add the details. You can start by drawing stick figures or round people. Begin by trying the cartoon figure below.

Stick figures

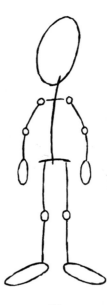

1 Draw a stick figure with oval head, hands, and feet. Put small circles at the joints.

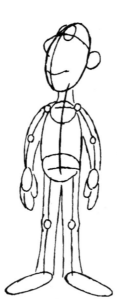

3 Draw in the basic **features** of the face.

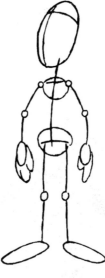

2 Build up the figure by adding more ovals for the body, such as for the shoulders and hips.

4 Finish by adding details for the face and clothing. Last of all, fill in with color.

TIP

You can use circles and ovals to make cartoon figures: stretched ovals make tall, skinny cartoons, circles make plump people. Mix the two to create fat people with spindly legs.

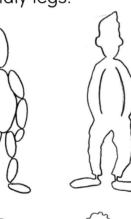

1 Draw the outline of your figure using circles or ovals.

2 Now add details to make them funny, such as hair, shoes, and clothes.

Big and little

To draw a cartoon of somebody you know, look at them carefully. Are they tall or short? Fat or thin? Now exaggerate their most outstanding feature. Practice drawing from photographs.

Faces and features

Faces and **expressions** are important in cartoons. Start at the top. First draw the head shapes, then add the different features. You can easily make your cartoon character look ahead or sideways.

Head on

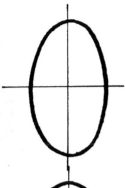

1 Draw an oval. Divide it into quarters.

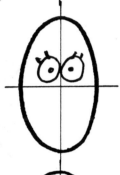

2 Put in the eyes just above the center.

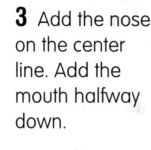

3 Add the nose on the center line. Add the mouth halfway down.

4 Add hair, eyebrows, and eyelashes. Make your faces happy, sad, or scared.

TIP

Try different face shapes: long and thin, short and fat! Fat heads have no neck. Thin heads look skinnier on a long, thin neck.

Hair can make a big difference to your characters. Different styles can make characters look messy or glamorous, young or old.

If you are making someone you know into a cartoon, look at them carefully. What do you notice most about them? Do they have a long chin? A wide face? Ears that stick out? A big nose? Glasses? These are the features you can exaggerate to make a great cartoon.

Remember glasses and jewelry. Details bring cartoons to life.

TIP

Look at your reflection in the back of a serving spoon. With your face in the light against a dark **background**, draw what you see. Your face will be stretched and distorted. Copy this for an instant cartoon effect.

Dressing up

The way you dress your cartoon characters helps to bring them to life. Uniforms and hats can tell you where their owners live, their job, or something about their personality.

Mix-and-match book

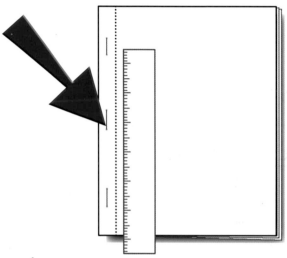

1 Staple six to eight sheets of unlined paper together to make a book. Draw a **vertical** line ¼ inch from the spine.

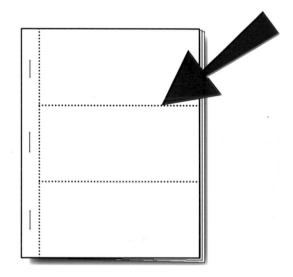

2 On the first page, using the ruler, divide the page into three equal **horizontal** sections.

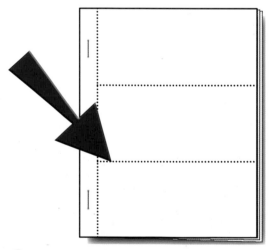

3 Ask an adult for help with this step. Cut along the horizontal lines as far as the vertical line, using scissors.

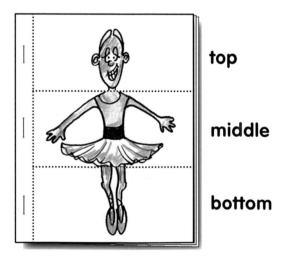

top

middle

bottom

4 Draw a cartoon character on the first page. Put the head and neck in the top third, the body in the middle, and the legs and feet in the bottom.

5 Flip back the middle section and mark where the neck and legs join the body on the next page. Use this as a guide for your next page.

6 Repeat the steps above. Flip the sections back and forward to make mixed-up cartoon characters!

On the move

Now you've created your cartoon characters, you need to make them move. Follow the hints and tips below to get them running, jumping, and even flying.

Action!

1 Begin with a simple stick figure.

2 Then add ovals and circles.

3 Now add clothes, color, and facial **expressions**.

Jumping

Running

Movement lines help to show which way something is moving—and how fast.

15

TIP

Movement lines also add extra action to your cartoon—just look at the pictures below. Adding double movement lines behind these figures makes them look more active.

Cartoon creatures

Before you start drawing cartoon animals, practice sketching real ones. Then try turning your sketches into cartoons.

Drawing animals

Notice the **features** and **personalities** of a variety of animals. A dog's ears can be droopy or perky, depending on whether it is happy or sad.

KOOKY ANIMALS

You can build up any kind of animal from simple shapes:

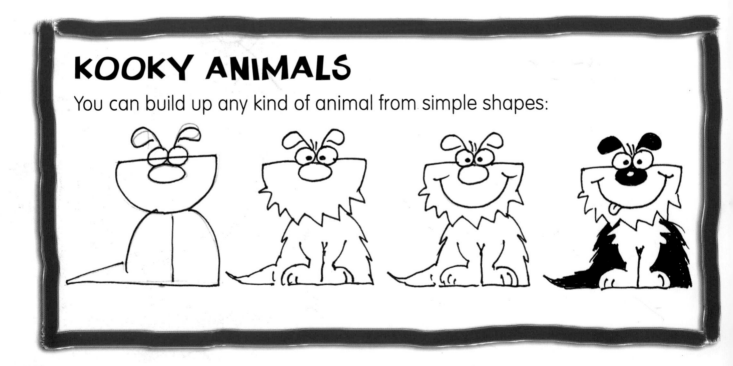

Animal shapes

1 Draw an **outline** of the head and body, using circles and ovals. Add the legs, feet, and tail.

2 Erase the guide lines that you don't want in the final picture.

3 Use colored pencils or pens to finish the drawing.

When you are confident about drawing animals, try stretching the body and limbs to make them taller and skinnier, or squash them for rounder, fatter, more comical, cartoon creatures.

PROJECT

Create a new animal star
Some animals have been turned into cartoons many times before—especially bears and cats! Try to think of something more unusual and see what you can do with it. Will it be fierce or friendly? Smart or stupid? Fast or slow?

It's alive!

Cartoons can make anything come to life. Look around your bedroom for inspiration—or your backyard or classroom. You can make your whole street into cartoon characters. The windows can be the eyes of the houses and the doors can be mouths.

Kitchen cartoons

Choose an object and get to know it well. Draw it so often, and from so many different angles, that it becomes as familiar as a friend.

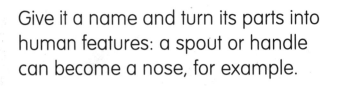

Give it a name and turn its parts into human features: a spout or handle can become a nose, for example.

Motor mouths

Give bikes, cars, scooters, skateboards, boats, trains, and buses funny faces to bring them to life. Try to make the shapes match the expressions—for example, a car can be round, smiley, and friendly or long, low, and aggressive, with a long radiator that looks like a mouthful of flashing teeth, and evil eyes instead of headlights.

Scary monsters

People, animals, buildings, or houses can make scary cartoons—and that's even before you start drawing the real monsters, such as vampires, werewolves, and ghosts!

Everyone will recognize a vampire. How about making up your own monsters?

Wicked witches are usually ugly and have pointed noses, long chins, and warts on their faces.

1   **2**   **3**

You can make ghosts as black **silhouettes**, or as white, cloudy shapes with a soft, black **outline** in the shape of a whirlwind.

MONSTER MIX UP

Try mixing parts of different animals into a new fantasy friend or **fiend**.

A question of size

Even tiny creatures can become terrifying if they grow to a huge size.

PROJECT

Mythical monsters

Myths and **legends** are full of strange and scary creatures, such as dragons, werewolves, and devils. Choose a mythical monster and turn it into a cartoon. Will yours be scary, friendly, or funny?

Set the scene

After you've created a group of cartoon characters, it's fun to put them in different **backgrounds**. Use real-life situations or invent a fantasy world—your background can be more interesting than a blank piece of paper.

TIP

Always start by sketching your cartoon character in soft pencil first, and then add the background. Add **foreground** details last. When you are happy with the finished result, color it in and go over the **outlines** in thick, black pen.

Where to get ideas

Look at travel magazines, photos, and books, or around your house, street, or school—which of these scenes suit your cartoon characters? Draw some simple backgrounds—choose a few details that show where the location is meant to be.

Placing your character

Your character should appear to be part of the scene, not just stuck on top of it—make sure that there is some detail in front of it as well as behind it.

Night or day?

Nighttime backgrounds are great for a spooky atmosphere. Draw your character and buildings in black **silhouette**.

IN THE MOOD

Different skies set the mood, too. It's easy to fill the sky with snow or rain!

Comic capers

Now that you've learned how to draw amazing cartoon figures, you can put them in your own comic story. First, take a look at some of your favorite comics. You'll see that the pages are split into **frames** of different sizes and shapes.

Frames don't have to be square! Try circles, ovals, and ones with jagged edges. You can draw the frames by hand so that they are not all straight lines or draw them neatly with a ruler. Comic strips look more exciting if parts of the picture break out of the frame edges.

Storylines

Your characters can "talk" in speech and thought bubbles. If you need extra information, and have enough space, you can put words in boxes at the top or bottom of the picture. Speech bubbles are usually oval. Bubbles that look like clouds are used to show a character's thoughts. Jagged bubbles are for angry people, and shivery bubbles can be used for a character who is scared.

Exclamation marks!

These punctuation marks are used a lot in comics! To show people shouting, use a thick black marker.

TIP

Speech and thought bubbles usually go in the top third of the picture, so draw your sketch in the bottom two-thirds.

25

Make a comic

Now that you've seen how it's done, try creating a comic strip with your own cast of funny, scary, or silly characters. You can even make a whole comicbook from a collection of strips.

YOUR CARTOON **CHARACTER** CAN DO **ANYTHING!**

Lights, camera, action!

Making a comic strip is like making a movie: you need a story, a main character, a few minor characters, and a series of **backgrounds**. Start by thinking up a short, simple story with a beginning, a middle, and an end. Look through some jokebooks for a funny ending.

Stars of the show

What will your main character look like? Decide what sort of **personality** they have and think of a name. Try drawing them from lots of different angles to get them right. You also need friends and enemies for the main character to talk to. Try not to have more than three characters, otherwise readers may get confused.

Storyboarding

You're ready to make a storyboard. This is a rough sketch of each frame; it doesn't have to be perfect. Try to vary the pictures. Sometimes characters can be in the distance, other times you can show a close-up of their face and **expression**.

Comic frames

When you are happy with your storyboard, turn it into a finished comic strip. Draw each box neatly, with a ruler and pencil. Make sure you draw the frames big enough to fit in all the details you want.

Finishing off

Copy your drawings from the storyboard and turn them into finished cartoons. First, draw the **outlines** in pencil.

Go over the outlines with black marker or felt-tip. Color in the pictures with paint or felt-tips. Your comic is complete!

Making movies

In an **animated** cartoon, thousands of pictures are shown at the rate of twenty-four pictures per second. This is too fast for our eyes, so we see a continual movement. If they were in an animated cartoon, these twelve pictures would appear on screen for just half a second.

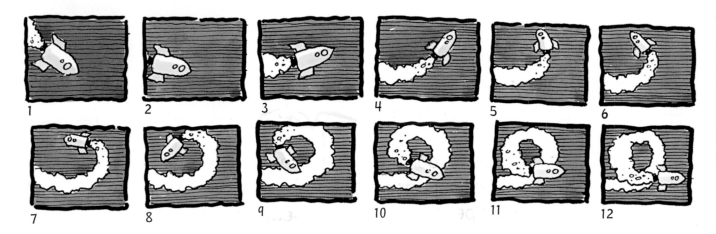

Make a flick book

Make a simple flick book to see your cartoons really move! You will need a small, unlined notebook and a pen or pencil. Decide what action you want to see animated—kicking a ball for example. Think about what you do when you kick a ball—try it out and see what your arms and legs do.

1 On a scrap of paper, from left to right, sketch about twenty stick figures. Change the position of the arms and legs slightly each time so that the figure really looks as if it is kicking a ball or walking.

2 Copy the first stick figure in the bottom corner of the first page.

3 Draw the second figure in the same place on the bottom corner of the next page. Keep going until you have drawn all the figures.

4 Bend the book slightly with your thumb at the edge and let the pages flick up. Your figure will appear to move! This is similar to how animated movies are made.

Try drawing different types of movement. Ask a friend to do the movements for you to copy or draw from your own reflection.

TIP

Animators use "key drawings" to work out a sequence of movements. If you want to draw someone running, jumping—or just drinking a cup of coffee— draw the start, middle, and end positions. These are your key drawings—now you can draw the sequences in between to link them.

Glossary

animated   images made to move by flashing lots of frames per second

B   soft pencil; even softer ones are marked 2B, 3B etc., up to 6B

background   things in the back of a picture, behind the main object

expressions   look on a person's face when they are happy, sad, puzzled, angry, etc.

features   ears, nose, eyes, and other parts of the face that make us all look different

fiend   an evil creature

foreground   area at the front of a picture

frames   boxes that make up a page in a comicbook

HB   medium pencil, harder pencils are marked 2H, 3H etc., to 6H

horizontal   across the page

legends   stories about the past

myths   stories about superhuman beings in the past

outline   outer edge of something

personality   way a person behaves

shade   to add dark areas to a picture

silhouette   object with just its outline visible and filled with a color

vertical   up and down the page

watercolors   paints that mix with water

Index

action 14–15
animals 6, 16–17
animated cartoon 28, 30

B pencils 4, 30
background 22–23, 30
bats 20

cars 19
characters 22–23, 26
circles 9, 14
comics 24–27

drawing board 4
dressing up 12–13

exaggeration 9, 11
exclamation marks 25
expressions 10–11, 19, 30

faces 10–11
fantasy characters 6
features 7, 10–11, 16, 30
felt-tips 4, 7, 27
flick book 28–29
foreground 22, 23, 30
frames 24, 27, 30

ghosts 21

hair 10, 11
HB pencils 4, 30
horizontal lines 12

inks 4, 7
inspiration 6, 18

jumping 14

key drawings 29

legends 21, 30
lighting 4
lines, showing movement 15

markers 4, 27
materials 4–5
monsters 6, 20–21
mood 23
movement 14–15
movies 28–29
myths 21, 30

nighttime 23

objects 6
    bringing alive 18–19
outlines 4, 7, 8, 17, 22, 24, 27, 30
ovals 9, 14

paints 4, 5, 27
paper 4
pencils 4, 5
pens 4, 5, 7

people 6, 7
    drawing figures 8–9
    dressing 12–13
    faces 10–11
    features 10–11
    shapes 9
personality 16, 30
photos 7
planes 19
poster paints 4
projects 17, 21
protecting work 4

running 14

shading 7, 30
silhouettes 21, 23, 30
size 21
skies 23
speech bubbles 25
stick figures 8, 14
stories 24–27
storylines 25
storyboarding 27

tools 4
trains 19

vampires 20
vertical lines 12

watercolors 4, 7, 30
witches 20
words 25

Notes for teachers and parents

The cartoon projects in this book can be used as stand-alone projects or as a part of other areas of study. While the ideas in the book are offered as inspiration, children should always be encouraged to draw from their imagination and first-hand observation.

Sourcing ideas

Whenever possible, art projects should tap into children's interests and be relevant to their lives and experiences. Try using stimulating starting points, such as friends, family, or pets, vacations, hobbies, television programs, or current affairs.

Encourage children to source their own ideas and references from comics, books, magazines, the Internet, or CD-ROM collections.

If you have access to a camcorder, ask the children to storyboard a simple animated cartoon sequence and video it frame by frame to see how well it works. Encourage the children to think of music and sound effects to go with their cartoon, as well as ways of making the instruments from everyday objects.

Cartoon images can also be created from other media, such as clay or Plasticine. These can be made into cartoons by using a video camera, moving the models each time you record a frame.

Use digital cameras to create reference material (landscapes, people, or animals) and use it next to the children's work (see below).

Other lessons can be an ideal springboard for a cartooning project—a school trip or a story from Greek mythology could be retold in picture-strip form. Get the children to look at the way that picture-book illustrators have used cartoon strips to retell history, legends, and stories from literature.

Encourage children to keep a sketchbook to draw their ideas, and to collect other images and objects to help them develop their cartoons.

Show the children a variety of animated cartoons, ranging from traditional and contemporary hand-drawn cartoons to computer-animated movies and the clay-model cartoons of Aardman Animations. The children can also look at a range of comicbooks, from simple comics aimed at toddlers to graphic novels.

Evaluating work

Children should share their work with others, and compare ideas and methods—this is often very motivating. Encourage them to talk about their work. How would they do it differently next time? What do they like best/least about the work?

Help children to judge the originality and value of their work, to appreciate the different qualities in others' work and different ways of working. Display all the children's work.

Discuss the use of different materials, such as felt tips, markers, inks, and watercolors. Experiment with different effects.

Going further

Look at ways to develop projects—for example, adapt the cartoons to make printed T-shirts, cards and pins, or characters for board games. Use image-enhancing computer software and digital scanners to enhance, build up, and juxtapose images in interesting and funny ways.

Work on a school comic, with a letters page, jokes, and competitions. Parents and children could pay a small amount to advertise in the comic.

Set up and develop a class cartoon gallery on your school website.